Anna L

Grace

Benjamin

Adonia

Daniel

Lewi

Isabella H

Thank you to Wellstead Primary School, Southampton
for helping with the endpapers.

For beautiful Oliver—V.T.

To Juliet Rose Jannes with love—K.P.

OXFORD
UNIVERSITY PRESS

Great Clarendon Street, Oxford OX2 6DP

Oxford University Press is a department of the University
of Oxford. It furthers the University's objective of excellence
in research, scholarship, and education by publishing worldwide.
Oxford is a registered trade mark of Oxford University Press in
the UK and in certain other countries

Text copyright © Valerie Thomas 2016
Illustrations copyright © Korky Paul 2016
The moral rights of the author and artist
have been asserted

Database right Oxford University Press (maker)

This edition first published in 2016

British Library Cataloguing in Publication Data available

ISBN: 978-0-19-274737-2 (hardback)

10 9 8 7 6 5 4 3 2 1

Printed in China

Paper used in the production of this book is a natural, recyclable
product made from wood grown in sustainable forests. The
manufacturing process conforms to the environmental
regulations of the country of origin

www.winnieandwilbur.com

VALERIE THOMAS AND KORKY PAUL

Winnie and Wilbur
MEET SANTA

OXFORD
UNIVERSITY PRESS

Winnie the Witch and her big black cat
Wilbur were getting ready for Christmas.
They loved Christmas. There was a lot to do.
Christmas cakes and
biscuits to make.

Christmas cards to write.

Christmas lights to string up.

And an enormous Christmas tree to decorate.
Luckily Winnie had her special Christmas spell.
She waved her magic wand, shouted,

'Abracadabra!'

and *everything* was ready.

Then Winnie and Wilbur
wrote their letters to Santa.
Wilbur wanted lots of things:
a wind up mouse,
tins of sardines,
a cuddly blanket, a . . .

'Don't be greedy, Wilbur,' Winnie said.
All she wanted was a lovely surprise.
She didn't mind what it was,
as long as it was a lovely surprise.

Fri 13 December
Dear Santa
All I want
is a
LOVELY-
SURPRISE.
Love
Winnie

They posted their letters to the North Pole.

On Christmas Eve Winnie and Wilbur felt very excited.
It was hard to go to sleep.
They were listening for reindeer on the roof.
But at last their eyes shut and they were asleep.

Winnie and Wilbur woke up.

CRASH!
BANG!
HELP! HELP!

What was all that noise?
They ran down the stairs, and there,
in the fireplace, was a big pair of black
boots and two red legs.

'Help me! I'm stuck!'
shouted a voice from
the chimney.
'It must be Santa!' said
Winnie. She grabbed
her magic wand, waved
it, and shouted,
'Abracadabra!'

There was a loud **pop** and Santa came out of the chimney. Santa was very pleased to see Winnie and Wilbur.

'I thought you'd never wake up,' he said.

'I've been stuck in that chimney for such a long time. But there are still lots and lots of presents to deliver. Will you help me?'

'Of course we will,' said Winnie. 'Come on, Wilbur.'

They rushed upstairs to get ready, and Santa popped their presents into the fireplace.

Then they climbed into Santa's sleigh and the reindeer flew high into the sky.

It was warm and snug in the sleigh, and the world beneath them looked so beautiful.

They flew over mountains and deserts, rivers and icebergs.

And everywhere there were sleeping children dreaming of their presents.

Santa was very good at delivering presents, but Winnie and Wilbur had problems.

Wilbur was chased by two playful puppies,

slipped into a Christmas stocking,

and was trapped in a cat flap.

Winnie wriggled into an igloo and then couldn't wriggle out.

She slid down a roof,

crashed into a cake, and got tangled in Christmas lights.

The reindeer parked the sleigh on top of a mountain. There were still lots and lots and lots of presents to deliver. 'Oh dear, oh dear!' said Santa. 'We'll never deliver all these presents before the children wake up. They will be so disappointed.' Big wet tears ran down Santa's rosy cheeks.

'We'll have to do something, Wilbur,' Winnie said. 'But what?' Then she had a wonderful idea. She would need very strong magic. Winnie shut her eyes, stood on tiptoe, waved her wand ten times, shouted,

'Abracadabra!'

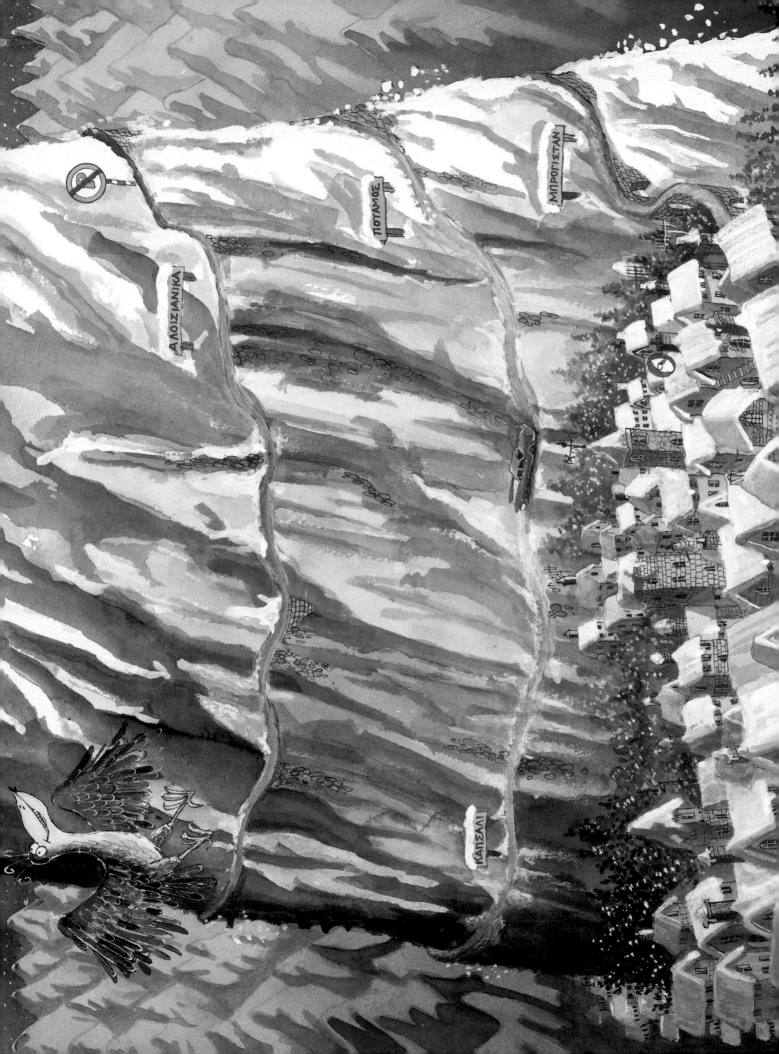

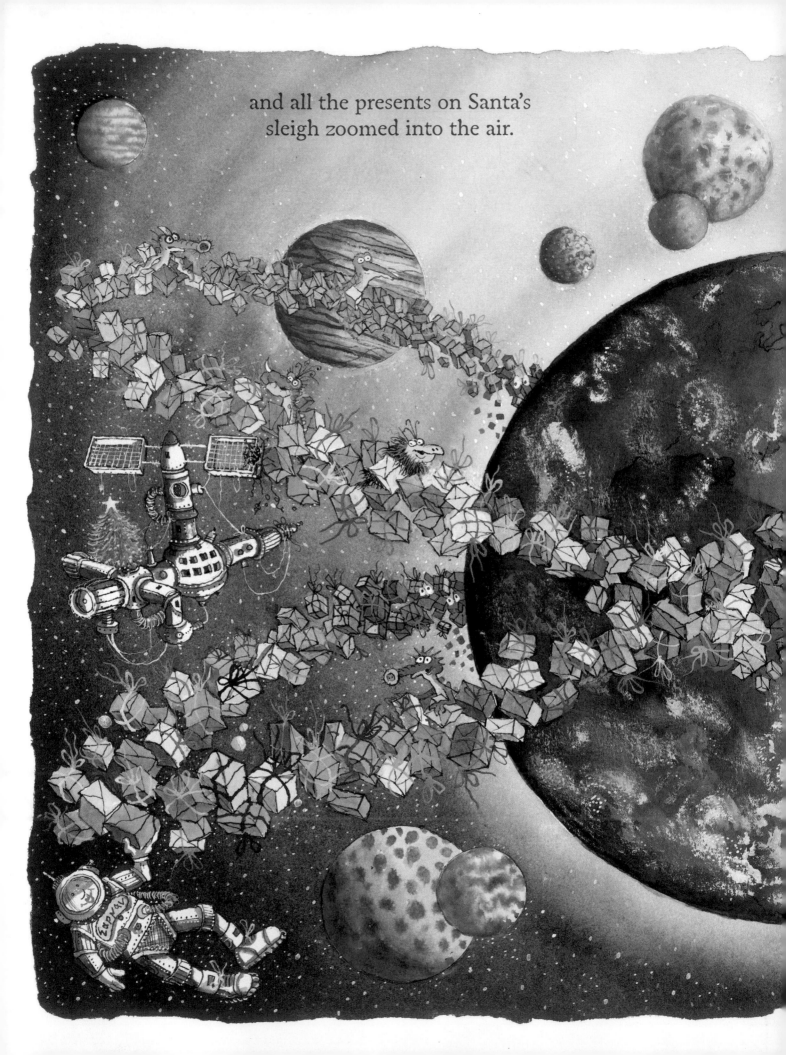

and all the presents on Santa's
sleigh zoomed into the air.

They flew like arrows around the world,
and all of the children had their presents.

'Thank you, Winnie and Wilbur,' Santa said.
'Now all the children will be happy.'

And he flew them home
to open their presents.

Wilbur had
lots of presents:
a wind up mouse,
tins of sardines,
a cuddly blanket, a . . .

There was just one present for Winnie.
An enormous present. What could it be?

'Ooooh!' said Winnie.
'Let's open it, Wilbur!'
They tore off the paper.

'Oooooh!' said Winnie.
'Isn't it wonderful, Wilbur!
Let's try it out right now.'
So they did.

And it was amazingly,
stupendously, fabulously, gloriously,
magnificently wonderful!

'We must say thank you to Santa, Wilbur,' Winnie said. So the next day they wrote a thank you letter.

Thursday 26 December
Dear Santa,